PENGUIN BOOKS

## ROTTEN REVIEWS II

Bill Henderson edits the *Pushcart Prize* series and has been known to write a book.

Anthony Brandt reviews books now and then and wrote the "Ethics" column for *Esquire*.

Mary Kornblum and her partner run Hudson Studio in Ossining, New York, where she designed this book and created the illustrations.

# ROTTEN
# REVIEWS
## —— II ——
### A · LITERARY · COMPANION

EDITED BY BILL HENDERSON

INTRODUCTION BY ANTHONY BRANDT
ILLUSTRATIONS BY MARY KORNBLUM

PENGUIN BOOKS

PENGUIN BOOKS
Published by the Penguin Group
Viking Penguin Inc., 40 West 23rd Street,
New York, New York 10010, U.S.A.
Penguin Books Ltd, 27 Wrights Lane, London W8 5TZ, England
Penguin Books Australia Ltd, Ringwood, Victoria, Australia
Penguin Books Canada Ltd, 2801 John Street,
Markham, Ontario, Canada L3R 1B4
Penguin Books (N.Z.) Ltd, 182–190 Wairau Road,
Auckland 10, New Zealand

Penguin Books Ltd, Registered Offices:
Harmondsworth, Middlesex, England

First published in the United States of America by
Pushcart Press 1987
Published in Penguin Books 1988

1 3 5 7 9 10 8 6 4 2

LIBRARY OF CONGRESS CATALOGING IN PUBLICATION DATA
Rotten reviews II: a literary companion/[edited by Bill Henderson].
p.   cm.
Reprint. Originally published: Wainscott, NY: Pushcart; New
York, NY: Distributed by Norton, © 1987.
ISBN 0 14 01.1248 0 (pbk.)
1. Books—Reviews.   2. Bibliography—Best books.   3. Books and
reading.   4. Literature, Modern—20th century—Book reviews.
I. Henderson, Bill, 1941–
Z1035.A1R68   1988
028.1—dc 19       88-17456

Printed in the United States of America by
Arcata Graphics, Kingsport, Tennessee
Set in Granjon

TO THE WRITER WHO SURVIVES ALL THIS;
AND TO THE FINAL CRITIC,
THE UNSUNG READER

*Selecting bad blurbs for last year's first edition of* Rotten Reviews *was rather simple. Certain books had come to be regarded as classics and all of these books had been bitterly resented at some time by reviewers.*

*Choosing contemporary titles to be represented in* Rotten Reviews II *has not been easy. Since we start more or less were* RR I *left off—1961—we do not have history to tell us what has endured. Instead we asked selected authors to contribute their favorite critic's snarls. Many did, with delight, and thus these authors had the last laugh, if not the last word, on their detractors.*

*We also scouted around for the really bitter blast—the review that is so malicious that it trips over itself.*

*Finally, we picked books and authors that remain a force in our time—even though enduring a few decades is not an especially remarkable feat when compared to the staying power of the classics of our first edition.*

*One of the delights in compiling this volume was the chance to hear from many authors with their opinions about the whole review process. A selection of their letters is included at the rear.*

*I do hope this edition will attract a few more lousy reviews than last year's. For some reason, the critics loved RRI. "A welcome bit of fun," said the* Philadelphia Inquirer. *The* Chicago Tribune *even went so far as to supply a few nasty notices from their pages that we had missed. The New York*

Times Book Review *ran a two page feature on our spoof.*

*In fact, the only rotten review for* Rotten Reviews #1 *arrived from a* TBR *reader who complained in the letters section: "Half the opinions are dead on target. The only things bad in Bill Henderson's compilation of bad blurbs are the assumptions a) that critical judgment makes any sense out of context b) that the general public in its infinite wisdom is always right."*

*That's the kind of response we like.*

*I would also like to thank Anthony Brandt for lending some weight to these light volumes in his thoughtful introductions. Tony once wrote the "Ethics" column for* Esquire *and knows about weighty matters. Thanks also to Mary Kornblum for designing and illustrating these pages.*

*And an appreciation also to the following authors who volunteered their meanest mentions for this edition: Edward Abbey, Margaret Atwood, Harold Brodkey, Amy Clampitt, Evan Connell, Annie Dillard, William Gaddis, Ken Gangemi, Allen Ginsberg, Edward Hoagland, David Ignatow, Erica Jong, Carolyn Kizer, Thomas McGrath, Jessica Mitford, Howard Nemerov, Joyce Carol Oates, Cynthia Ozick, Leon Rooke, May Sarton, Lynne Sharon Schwartz, William Stafford, Wallace Stegner, Thomas Szasz and Paul West.*

*We expect that many of our readers will be examining this volume in a secluded, small room (see Ansel Adams' letter to Wallace Stegner at the back) and we think this is appropriate.*

BILL HENDERSON

*Sweet, bland commendations fall everywhere upon the scene. A book is born into a puddle of treacle; the brine of hostile criticism is only a memory.*

ELIZABETH HARDWICK

"Contemporary criticism," wrote the great Shelley, "only represents the amount of ignorance genius has to contend with." And: "Time will reverse the judgement of the vulgar." It is a comforting thought, and it is sometimes true. Did reviewers almost universally dismiss *The Great Gatsby* when it first appeared? Now Departments of English all over the country teach it as an American classic. Was Melville driven out of literature by his multitudinous critics? Now I participate every year, along with thirty or forty other people, in a marathon public reading of *Moby Dick* that our local bookseller puts on. The good must in the end drive out the bad. Gresham's Law does not apply to the economy of literature.

Or so we would like to believe. But is the destiny of good writing always so benign? Could it be that public taste is as subject to whim, to fashion, to chance over the long run as it is in the short? And what writer is such a philosopher or so confident of his worth that he can wait serenely for the judgment of the ages in any case? What writer would not openly prefer to be famous now, when he can enjoy it? When it might well make him rich?

Rotten reviews: they are amusing in the context of time. We smile when Dr. Johnson condemns the poetry of John Donne, or Henry James waves off Emily Bronte. Even great men, it seems, can be spectacularly wrong. But the amusement has no edge. We know perfectly well

11

that Donne and Bronte survived in spite of their critics. Donne's poetry is still taught at the universities; people still read *Wuthering Heights* with pleasure. For contemporary writers, however—and this collection consists only of the reviews of contemporary writers—no such future is assured. People may be reading Joe Heller's novels in 2087, or they may not. *The Listener*'s witty remark at May Sarton's expense, recorded here, may well outlast May Sarton. These are living writers and we have not yet (if you will forgive the expression) closed the books on them.

One cannot, therefore, help but admire those writers (like May Sarton) who actually submitted examples of bad reviews to this collection. What good sports! One cannot help but sympathize with those who declined the honor. These reviews are funny, but they also hurt. Malcolm Cowley reported recently how he felt when his own classic (we know now), *Exile's Return*, appeared in 1934 to widespread condemnation, particularly among older, more influential reviewers: "It all seems amusing in retrospect, but the impression it gave me of being exposed and helpless, a criminal chained and taunted in the marketplace, was a shattering experience while it lasted. . . . I reviewed for the *New Republic*—with rather more kindness to authors than I had shown in the beginning, I wrote essays and poems, but for years I couldn't bring myself to write another book."

Nor is it only a matter of hurt feelings. *Exile's Return* sold a mere 983 copies in the year of Cowley's agony. It did not do well until 1951, when Viking reissued it. In the light of eternity the writer's concern for his income may seem laughable and petty. Up close, with the rent due and nothing but a jar of olive oil in the cupboard, a rotten review can do more than hurt, it can send a writer over the edge. Into bricklaying, say. Or worse, public relations. And this may be a very good writer. One whom destiny may someday have chosen as one of her darlings.

If writers are sensitive about their reviews, then, or if they or their publishers even resort at times to less than ethical stratagems to guarantee that they will be favorable, be not surprised. In the book trade, the sensitivity of writers is taken for granted and gossip about such stratagems is common. And examples from history abound. In January of 1836 S. G. Goodrich, editor, publisher, and sometime writer, arranged for Nathaniel Hawthorne to assume the editorship of the *American Magazine of Useful and Entertaining Knowledge*. The relationship between the two men was troubled, however, and by February 15 Hawthorne was furious with Goodrich, who owed him $46 for several contributions to one of the gift book annuals Goodrich published. Hawthorne had 34 cents in his pocket at the time and was forced to borrow money from his sister, whom he told that he had broken off "all intercourse" with Goodrich. Then, four days later, Goodrich paid up. He also sent Hawthorne two copies of his book of poems, *The Outcast*. Would Hawthorne perhaps review the book for one of the Boston papers? Four days after that Hawthorne's review of Goodrich's egregious poems appeared in the *Boston Daily Atlas*.

It was a favorable review.

*The Outcast*, needless to say, has not survived the test of time.

What shall we say about this? That Hawthorne high-mindedly put aside his less than generous feelings about S. G. Goodrich to praise a book in which he found real merit? Or that he knew which side his bread was buttered on? What shall we say about Goodrich, asking a writer he in effect employed to write a review of his book? What shall we say, indeed, about the well-known contemporary novelist who, when he was a resident at a well-known writers' colony, became involved with an unknown writer, then, when her book finally appeared, wrote a rave review and made her a star?

It need not go this way, of course. I know a case where malice operated as effectively as love. A writer who had won a National Magazine Award for one of his articles expanded it into a book. The person who reviewed his book for another major literary organ was one of the finalists he had defeated for the National Magazine Award. He did not get a rave review. I myself have written favorable reviews of books in which friends of mine had an interest, either as author or publisher. The reviews were honest—i.e., I liked the books—but no doubt I was predisposed to like them. The world of letters is a small one. Like a small town it is full of both friends and enemies. People who may well be friends or enemies are frequently asked to review each other's books. The writer has little or no control over which it shall be. And a great deal is at stake: money, reputation, whole careers. In

1806 the poet Thomas Moore became so enraged over a rotten review of his *Odes and Epistles* in the *Edinburgh Review* that he challenged the reviewer, a man named Jeffrey, to a duel. The two men, neither of whom had any experience with pistols, were only stopped from going through with it at the last moment, when several policemen arrived on the scene and arrested them.

Rotten reviews: we smile; we are amused; but we should be aware of what is at stake, and we should have some sense of what goes on behind the scenes. A powerful editor at a powerful publishing house can often not only get a book reviewed, he can occasionally influence the tone of that review. Writers sometimes ask friends, without their acknowledging to the reviewing organ that they are friends, to review their books. (This doesn't always work. In 1930 Yvor Winters, with whom Hart Crane had been carrying on a mutually supportive correspondence for years, reviewed Crane's book *The Bridge* in the influential journal *Poetry* and, to Crane's horror, tore it apart.) People who have reason to dislike other people intensely sometimes arrange to review their books. Occasionally book review editors will knowingly assign reviews to enemies of the writers being reviewed.

If all this sounds less than ethical, well, nobody ever said that reviewing was the world's most ethical profession. Sometimes, indeed, it seems more like jungle warfare. "Like politics," writes the sociologist Levin L. Schucking, "the life of art consists of a struggle to enlist followers." It is a struggle with booby traps. Talent, even greatness are no guarantees of success. Not only must the writer contend with the indifference of his peers or their failure to comprehend him, he must master the politics of the literary world. He is in competition with thousands of other writers trying to do the same thing, many of whom would be only too happy for the chance to review his books. He may have enemies he does not know are enemies. And after years of effort, the heart-breaking labor that could be his life's work, it may all be over in a few well-chosen words.

That having been said, it remains to point out that this collection is still a good deal of fun to read. Writers need a sense of humor or they could not survive at all. "The author of this book should be neutered and locked away forever," writes the *San Juan County Record* of Edward Abbey's *The Monkey Wrench Gang*. Abbey himself, bless his heart, sent this outrageous nugget in. Reviewers can be malicious; they can also be witty. Whatever we may feel for the authors, it is hard not to take a certain amount of pleasure in both the wit and the malice.

And why not? Let's be honest. Some, at least, of the books reviewed here will not last. Some of the reputations of the writers reviewed here will prove over the years to have been, shall we say, inflated. Time will not always reverse the judgment of the vulgar, as Shelley hoped; it will sometimes confirm it. Some of these reviews, in short, will echo what we ourselves may think of the books in question, or of their authors. Americans love to trash the mighty, and those who aspire to be mighty have to get used to it. So large an ego as Norman Mailer's, say, or Allen Ginsberg's is certainly up to the punishment. If reviewing is a kind of warfare, it is one that makes for a fine spectator sport.

And it is not, finally, just for their value as fun that we should be grateful for rotten reviews. While nobody wants to read only what the times approve, we cannot read everything, and some books are so bad, such complete wastes of our finite spans of attention (no matter how well-known the writers that produced them), that the need for some system to winnow them out is self-evident. Good intentions are not enough to make a good book; talent is sparingly distributed—why should the world pretend otherwise?

All this goes without saying; I mention it only because there are people who think there should be no rotten reviews. On the contrary, we clearly need them. Perhaps even writers need them: as a test of courage, of faith in their own abilities; as a spur, perhaps, to tough-mindedness. Here is what Jean Cocteau had to say on the subject: "Listen carefully to first criticisms of your work. Note just what it is about your work that critics don't like—then cultivate it. That's the part of your work that's individual and worth keeping."

ANTHONY BRANDT

ROTTEN REVIEWS II

### THE MONKEY WRENCH GANG
EDWARD ABBEY
1975

The author of this book should be neutered and locked away forever.

*San Juan County Record*

### ABBEY'S ROAD
EDWARD ABBEY
1978

If you want to read 200 pages of Edward Abbey's self-flattery buy this . . . smug, graceless book.

*The New Republic*

### COUNTING THE WAYS
EDWARD ALBEE
1977

. . . the play sounds like George Burns and Gracie Allen trying to keep up a dinner conversation with Wittgenstein . . . I have never seen such desperately ingratiating smiles on the faces of actors.

*Newsweek*

## A WALK ON THE WILD SIDE
### NELSON ALGREN
### 1956

. . . my, how this boy needs editing!

*San Francisco Chronicle*

## ONE FAT ENGLISHMAN
### KINGSLEY AMIS
### 1964

. . . fatty is not only a boor, but a bore, and that quickly makes the satire a matter of satiety.

*America*

## THE HANDMAID'S TALE
### MARGARET ATWOOD
### 1986

Norman Mailer, wheezing lewd approval of some graphic images he encountered in the writing of Germaine Greer, remarked that 'a wind in this prose whistled up the kilt of male conceit.' Reading Margaret Atwood, I don my kilt but the wind never comes. Just a cold breeze.

*The American Spectator*

Reader checks reviewer's kilt.

## GIOVANNI'S ROOM
### JAMES BALDWIN
### 1956

No matter of careful recording of detail or of poetic heightening of feeling can supply what is absent here—the understanding which is vital whether a character in fiction merely takes a walk or commits incest . . .

*Commonweal*

## THE SOTWEED FACTOR
### JOHN BARTH
### 1961

. . . too long, too long, too long.

*New York Herald Tribune*

## GILES GOAT-BOY
### JOHN BARTH
### 1966

. . . a pervasive silliness that turns finally—if one must bring up the university image—into college humor, a kind of MAD magazine joke.

*Christian Science Monitor*

## LOVE ALWAYS
### ANN BEATTIE
### 1985

. . . Beattie's admirable eye for the telling detail has unfortunately developed a squint . . .

*Commonweal*

## HOW IT IS
### SAMUEL BECKETT
### 1964

. . . he breeds nothing but confusion. His plays and novels present a vision of life that is shockingly unchristian. They make the life and death of our Lord just one more of the legends man has used to delude himself . . . Beckett is postulating this as our inescapable condition of life. It may be for him. Not for this reader.

R.H. Glauber, *Christian Century*

## THE ADVENTURES OF AUGIE MARCH
### SAUL BELLOW
### 1953

All of Those Words, in denominations of from three to five letters, are present.

*Library Journal*

## HENDERSON THE RAIN KING
SAUL BELLOW
1959

The novelist who doesn't like meanings writes an allegory; the allegory means that men should not mean but be. Ods bodkins. The reviewer looks at the evidence and wonders if he should damn the author and praise the book, or praise the author and damn the book. And is it possible, somehow or other to praise or damn, both? He isn't sure.

Reed Whittemore, *New Republic*

At times Henderson is too greyly overcast with thought to be more than a dun Quixote.

*Time*

## HERZOG
SAUL BELLOW
1961

There is no effort toward decency—many of the conversations that come back to Herzog are foul-mouthed, and his own sexual actions and reminiscences are unrestrained.

*America*

### LITTLE BIG MAN
THOMAS BERGER
1964

. . . a farce that is continually over-reaching itself. Or, as the Cheyenne might put it, Little Big Man Little Overblown.

Gerald Walker, *New York Times Book Review*

### THE MAN WHO KNEW KENNEDY
VANCE BOURJAILY
1967

The man who knew Kennedy didn't know him very well. I'm almost as intimate with Lyndon Johnson. I met him once.

Webster Schott, *New York Times Book Review*

### WOMEN AND ANGELS
HAROLD BRODKEY
1985

. . . much of it reads like an extended obituary produced by a team of more than usually fanciful computers.

*New York Review of Books*

## A CLOCKWORK ORANGE
### ANTHONY BURGESS
### 1963

. . . 'The holy bearded veck all nagoy hanging on a cross' is an example of the author's language and questionable taste. . . . The author seems content to use a serious social challenge for frivolous purposes, but himself to stay neutral.

*Times* (London)

## THE TICKET THAT EXPLODED
### WILLIAM BURROUGHS
### 1967

The works of William Burroughs . . . have been taken seriously, even solemnly, by some literary types, including Mary McCarthy and Norman Mailer. Actually, Burroughs's work adds up to the world's pluperfect put-on.

*Time*

## NAKED LUNCH
### WILLIAM BURROUGHS
### 1963

. . . the merest trash, not worth a second look.

*New Republic*

## NOVA EXPRESS
### WILLIAM BURROUGHS
### 1964

. . . The book is unnecessary.

Granville Hicks, *Saturday Review*

## IN COLD BLOOD
### TRUMAN CAPOTE
### 1965

One can say of this book—with sufficient truth to make it worth saying: 'This isn't writing. It's research.'

Stanley Kauffmann, *The New Republic*

## WHAT WE TALK ABOUT WHEN WE TALK ABOUT LOVE
### RAYMOND CARVER
### 1980

There is nothing here to appease a reader's basic literary needs.

*Atlantic Monthly*

## CASTLE TO CASTLE
### LOUIS FERDINAND CÉLINE
### 1969

. . . quite a tedious book.

John Weightman, *New York Review of Books*

## THE WAPSHOT SCANDAL
### JOHN CHEEVER
### 1964

Fatally flawed.

Hilary Corke, *New Republic*

## WHAT THE LIGHT WAS LIKE
### AMY CLAMPITT
### 1985

. . . it would be better for Amy Clampitt if, at least for a while, she tucked her notes from Poetry 101 away in a trunk.

*Poetry*

### MRS. BRIDGE
EVAN CONNELL
1959

It's hard to believe that a lady from Kansas City with a house in the best residential section, one full-time maid, one mink coat and a Lincoln for her very own, should finish up as timorous and ephemeral as a lunar moth on the outside of a window.

Florence Crowther, *New York Times Book Review*

### NOTES FROM A BOTTLE FOUND ON THE BEACH AT CARMEL
EVAN CONNELL
1963

. . . almost pure gingerbread. It has bite, a certain flavor, but it turns into a gluey mass when chewed.

*San Francisco Examiner*

### MR. BRIDGE
EVAN CONNELL
1969

It is hard to imagine a creep like Bridge ever lived. If he did, so what? Connell fails to show that he has any relevance to what's happening in America, 1969.

*Cleveland Press*

A novel should be something more than an X-ray of a dull life.

*Bridgeport Post*

## SON OF MORNING STAR
### EVAN CONNELL
### 1985

Unfortunately, the big story often seems to elude Connell, who is obsessed with digression, flashback and flashforward.

*Commentary*

This do-it-yourself kit will appeal to those who think confusion is a narrative strategy.

J.O. Tate, *National Review*

## THE ORIGIN OF THE BRUNISTS
### ROBERT COOVER
### 1966

. . . an explosion in a cesspool.

Bruno McAndrew, *Best Sellers*

## THE PUBLIC BURNING
### ROBERT COOVER
### 1977

. . . an overwritten bore . . . a protracted sneer.

Paul Gray, *Time*

## GERALD'S PARTY
### ROBERT COOVER
### 1986

The Novel should develop a reader's sensitivities, not deaden them with risible comic-strip.

*New Statesman*

## SALVADOR
### JOAN DIDION
### 1983

. . . she makes the tiny republic of El Salvador into a mirror reflecting her own basic contempt for liberal democracy and—why not say it?—the American Way of Life.

*Commentary*

## PILGRIM AT TINKER CREEK
### ANNIE DILLARD
### 1974

I have never seen frogs in Virginia 'shout and glare' . . .

Loren Eiseley, *Washington Post Book World*

## THE GINGER MAN
### J.P. DONLEAVY
### 1958

Disgust, indignation, and boredom—those are the most likely responses to be anticipated among readers of *The Ginger Man*. No doubt the book will also get a few screams of praise from those who habitually confuse the effects of art with the effects of shock and sensation . . . This rather nasty, rather pompous novel gives us, in all, a precocious small boy's view of life, the boy having been spoiled somehow and allowed to indulge in sulks and tantrums and abundant self-pity.

*Chicago Tribune*

## 10:30 ON A SUMMER NIGHT
### MARGUERITE DURAS
### 1963

. . . has the proud air of saying in her every painful, glottal line, 'Hup for prose!'

Hortense Calisher, *The Nation*

## INVISIBLE MAN
### RALPH ELLISON
### 1952

It has its faults which cannot simply be shrugged off—
occasional overwriting, stretches of fuzzy thinking, and
a tendency to waver, confusingly, between realism and
surrealism.

*Atlantic Monthly*

## A FAN'S NOTES
### FREDERICK EXLEY
### 1968

The book's fault is its lack of passion.

*Library Journal*

## LOVE AND DEATH IN THE
## AMERICAN NOVEL
### LESLIE FIEDLER
### 1960

The author can't win, ever, by Fiedler's standard of judgment. Only the critic can win. . . . There is more in
American fiction, much more, than Fiedler has been able
to find.

Malcolm Cowley, *New York Times Book Review*

## THE FEMININE MYSTIQUE
### BETTY FRIEDAN
### 1963

. . . It is a pity that Mrs. Friedan has to fight so hard to persuade herself as well as her readers of her argument. In fact her passion against the forces of the irrational in life quite carries her away.

*Yale Review*

It is superficial to blame the 'culture' and its handmaidens, the women's magazines, as she does . . . To paraphrase a famous line, 'the fault dear Mrs. Friedan, is not in our culture, but in ourselves.'

*New York Times Book Review*

## THE RECOGNITIONS
### WILLIAM GADDIS
### 1955

*The Recognitions* is an evil book, a scurrilous book, a profane book, a scatological book and an exasperating book. . . . what this squalling overwritten book needs above all is to have its mouth washed out with lye soap. It reeks of decay and filth and perversion and half-digested learning.

*Chicago Sun Times*

## JR
### WILLIAM GADDIS
### 1976

To produce an unreadable text, to sustain this foxy purpose over 726 pages, demands rare powers. Mr. William Gaddis has them.

George Steiner, *The New Yorker*

JR is Gaddis's second novel, is like nothing else around, and is not a masterpiece.

Alfred Kazin, *New Republic*

(Gaddis) dumps everything into these pages except what they most desperately need—the ironic and flexible detachment of a discriminating mind.

Pearl K. Bell, *The New Leader*

## OLT
### KENNETH GANGEMI
### 1970

Really the most interesting part is the jacket information that Gangemi was born in Scarsdale, took an engineering degree at R.P.I. . . . .

William Pritchard, *Hudson Review*

## MICKELSSON'S GHOSTS
### JOHN GARDNER
### 1982

. . . dreadfully long and padded and it often degenerates into drivel . . . as a philosophical novel, it is a sham. Stripped of its excesses, however, it does not have enough substance to have made a good Raymond Carver short story.

*Saturday Review*

## THE WRECKAGE OF AGATHON
### JOHN GARDNER
### 1970

'Wreckage' is appropriate . . . more hysterical than historical.

*Library Journal*

## OCTOBER LIGHT
### JOHN GARDNER
### 1977

Within this great welter of words, symbols and gassy speechifying and half-hatched allegory there was once, I suspect, a good lean novel, but I can't find it . . .

Peter Prescott, *Newsweek*

## OMENSETTER'S LUCK
### WILLIAM H. GASS
### 1966

. . . Gass has not a particle of the savoir-faire of Faulkner. The pages ramble on, almost devoid of dialogue. This first novel is not for the reader longing for a good story narrative.

*Library Journal*

## IN THE HEART OF THE HEART OF THE COUNTRY
### WILLIAM H. GASS
### 1968

The publisher promises that anyone who has a deep love for the well-made English sentence will find these stories richly rewarding. Perhaps so. But there is every chance that the rest of us—those who prefer to curl up with a good book—will be left gasping with boredom instead.

*Book World*

## HOWL AND OTHER POEMS
### ALLEN GINSBERG
### 1956

It is only fair to Allen Ginsberg . . . to remark on the utter lack of decorum of any kind in his dreadful little volume . . . 'Howl' is meant to be a noun, but I can't help taking it as an imperative.

John Hollander, *Partisan Review*

## THE PERFECTIONISTS
### GAIL GODWIN
### 1971

. . . the men are all fatuous and self-centered creatures. This is then a woman's novel in a narrow and constricting way.

*Saturday Review*

## THE ODD WOMAN
### GAIL GODWIN
### 1974

A generous, sensitive, intelligent, humane and literate book that despite its generosity, sensitivity, humanity, and literacy, manages to be a deadly bore.

*The New Yorker*

## A MOTHER AND TWO DAUGHTERS
GAIL GODWIN
1981

Godwin earnestly sticks by her characters ... The only trouble is, like the people next door, they're nice but not very interesting.

*Saturday Review*

## LORD OF THE FLIES
WILLIAM GOLDING
1955

... completely unpleasant.

*The New Yorker*

## GROWING UP ABSURD
PAUL GOODMAN
1961

The worst written book I have read in quite a long time.

D.W. Brogan, *The Guardian*

## THE TIN DRUM
### GÜNTER GRASS
#### 1963

Bewildered by the torrent of fantastic incident, mystified by what Günter Grass intends by it all, one feels like a zoologist who discovers some monstrous unrecorded mammal gobbling leaves: It may have beautiful horns, but what is it?

*New Statesman*

## THE FEMALE EUNUCH
### GERMAINE GREER
#### 1971

Bores aid no revolution.

*Library Journal*

## WEBSTER'S THIRD NEW INTERNATIONAL DICTIONARY OF THE ENGLISH LANGUAGE
### PHILIP BABCOCK GROVE, EDITOR
#### 1962

. . . a copyeditor's despair, a propounder of endless riddles.

*Atlantic Monthly*

## WE BOMBED IN NEW HAVEN
### JOSEPH HELLER
### 1968

A dud of the first magnitude . . .

*Saturday Review*

## SOMETHING HAPPENED
### JOSEPH HELLER
### 1974

. . . surely it's time to declare a moratorium on brain-damaged children used as metaphors for mental and emotional decay.

*Library Journal*

## GOOD AS GOLD
### JOSEPH HELLER
### 1979

. . . a self-indulgent ventilation of private spleen . . . Heller operates as if he were a jewel thief wearing boxing gloves.

*Newsweek*

## TOYS IN THE ATTIC
### LILLIAN HELLMAN
1961

It is curious how incest, impotence, nymphomania, religious mania and real estate speculation can be so dull.

Richard Findlater, *Time and Tide*

Lillian Hellman has chosen to write on a Tennessee Williams theme in an Agatha Christie style.

*Times* (London)


## SCOUNDREL TIME
### LILLIAN HELLMAN
1977

*Scoundrel Time* is historically a fraud, artistically a put-up job and emotionally packed with meanness.

Dwight MacDonald, *Esquire*


## A MOVEABLE FEAST
### ERNEST HEMINGWAY
1964

Judging by this memoir, it would seem the Hemingway estate is prepared to dribble out some very small beer indeed in the name of the master. This book was apparently completed in Cuba in 1960 and, for all the good it is likely to do Hemingway's reputation, it could very well have stayed there—permanently . . .

Geoffrey Wagner, *Commonweal*

## CAT MAN
### EDWARD HOAGLAND
### 1956

This lengthy description of the lower depths of existence among men who pick up a living around travelling circuses is frequently disgusting in an eager, repetitious, small-boy way.

*The New Yorker*

## THE DEPUTY
### ROLF HOCHHUTH
### 1964

*The Deputy* on Broadway is like one of those comic-strip versions of a literary classic . . . and as the characters bestride the stage you can virtually see the balloons coming out of their mouths.

John Simon, *Hudson Review*

## POEMS 1934-1969
### DAVID IGNATOW
### 1970

Milch-poems I'd call them, reliable for uniform milk.

*Chicago Tribune*

## NEW AND COLLECTED POEMS: 1970-1985
### DAVID IGNATOW
### 1986

A reader prone to despondency had better steel himself before encountering David Ignatow's poems—or avoid them, unless he believes in homeopathy.

*Poetry*

## THE HOTEL NEW HAMPSHIRE
### JOHN IRVING
### 1981

Eager to reassure us that his novel is all in good fun despite the bloody goings-on, Irving resorts to a gee-whiz idiom right out of 'Leave It To Beaver.'

James Atlas, *New York Times Book Review*

Dave Ignatow had a farm...

. . . not only a confusing but a boring novel . . . John Irving ought to quit wasting his time . . .

*The Nation*

## FEAR OF FLYING
### ERICA JONG
### 1974

This crappy novel, misusing vulgarity to the point where it becomes purely foolish, picturing women as a hapless organ animated by the simplest ridicule, and devaluing imagination in every line . . . represents everything that is to be loathed in American fiction today.

Paul Theroux, *New Statesman*

## LEGS
### WILLIAM KENNEDY
### 1975

. . . a made for TV book. Consult your local listings for time and station.

*Library Journal*

## CONTEMPORARIES
### ALFRED KAZIN
### 1962

This critic is a man who knows all there is to know about literature except how to enjoy it . . .

Nelson Algren, *The Nation*

## ON THE ROAD
### JACK KEROUAC
### 1957

He can slip from magniloquent hysteria into sentimental bathos, and at his worst he merely slobbers words . . . a writer to watch, but if this watching is to be rewarded, he must begin to watch himself.

*Chicago Tribune*

## ONE FLEW OVER THE CUCKOO'S NEST
### KEN KESEY
### 1962

Kesey builds up an atmosphere of real horror and significance and then dispels it ineffectively with some quite misplaced slapstick. The book never gets back firmly on the track and a flurry of activity at the end isn't quite lively enough to disguise the fact that it's getting nowhere.

*Commonweal*

## THE WHITE HOUSE YEARS
### HENRY KISSINGER
### 1979

Doctor Henry Kissinger has constructed a diplomacy for a Hobbesian world . . . When he exercised that diplomacy he helped create the kind of world that would justify it.

*New Republic*

## MIDNIGHT WAS MY CRY
### CAROLYN KIZER
### 1971

Like most poets, she teaches, and like most teachers, she isn't very good.

*Esquire*

## THE GOLDEN NOTEBOOK
### DORIS LESSING
### 1962

The novel is a ponderous bore.

Julian Mitchell, *The Spectator*

Few readers will want to subject themselves to the demands of this huge complex and ugly book ... The apparatus becomes tiresome, the obscenities and clinical language depressing; the occasional satisfactions of seeing how bits of the puzzle fit together are not enough.

*Christian Science Monitor*

## ADVERTISEMENT FOR MYSELF
NORMAN MAILER
1960

The book as a whole shapes up as a manifesto of a writer on his way out. . . . The plain fact is that, soured by what he interprets as 'defeat' at the hands of 'a most loathsome literary world, necrophilic to the core,' Mailer has chosen to be a literary terrorist.

*Atlantic Monthly*

. . . a record of an artistic crackup.

*Time*

## AN AMERICAN DREAM
NORMAN MAILER
1965

Mailer meant to make money with this book. Hollywood should go for it. It should make the Best Seller lists. But it is a book calculated to leave All America holding its nose.

*Best Sellers*

Not for a moment can the novel be taken seriously as a portrayal of life in America—or anywhere else . . . I should like to believe the novel is a hoax.

Granville Hicks, *Saturday Review*

### WHY ARE WE IN VIETNAM?
NORMAN MAILER
1967

. . . a third rate work of art, but it's a first rate outrage to our sensibilities.

Anatole Broyard, *New York Times Book Review*

### THE GROUP
MARY MCCARTHY
1963

The McCarthy lode is petering out.

*America*

. . . a minor achievement and a major disappointment.

Stanley Kauffmann, *New Republic*

### BIRDS OF AMERICA
MARY MCCARTHY
1971

. . . a weight watcher's erotic dream and Miss McCarthy's most saporific fiction yet.

Peter Prescott, *Newsweek*

## "UNDERGROUND"
### THOMAS MCGRATH
### 1986

. . . barbaric yawps.

Kirkus Reviews

## TROPIC OF CAPRICORN
### HENRY MILLER
### 1962
#### FIRST PUBLISHED IN PARIS, 1939

. . . a flamboyant failure.

*San Francisco Chronicle*

. . . a gadfly with delusions of grandeur.

*Time*

## TAR BABY
### TONI MORRISON
### 1981

Heavy-handed, and ultimately unintelligible . . . topples into dreadful pits of bombast.

*The New Yorker*

## THE AMERICAN WAY OF DEATH
### JESSICA MITFORD
### 1963

While hiding behind the commercial aspects of the mortician and the cemeteries and mausoleums where our

Congressman hunts Commies.

dear departed friends and relatives are commemorated, she is really striking another blow at the Christian religion. Her tirade against morticians is simply the vehicle to carry her anti-Christ attack . . . I would rather place my mortal remains, alive or dead, in the hands of any American mortician than to set foot on the soil of any Communist nation.

Congressman James B. Utt, *Congressional Record*

## PALE FIRE
### VLADIMIR NABOKOV
### 1962

Perhaps for some tastes the verbal display and the internal trickery will be sufficient to outweigh the uncleanness that almost seems to stick to the reader's hands. Others, like this reader, may consider *Pale Fire* a prodigal waste of its author's gifts.

Roderick Nordell, *Christian Science Monitor*

## A HOUSE FOR MR. BISWAS
### V.S. NAIPAUL
### 1962

Naipaul's House, though built of excellent exotic materials, sags badly; economy, style, and a less elastic blueprint would have done wonders.

*Time*

## THE OAK IN THE ACORN
### HOWARD NEMEROV
### 1987

. . . fairly feeble attempt to explain Proust . . . an unilluminating exercise in Marcel-worship.

Kirkus Reviews

## THEM
### JOYCE CAROL OATES
### 1969

. . . earnestly out of it . . . her version of what people feel now in the inner city in riot areas is as naive as a proto-Martian's might be.

*Library Journal*

## ON BOXING
### JOYCE CAROL OATES
### 1987

Clearly this represents an attempt by a purely feminine psyche to come to terms with the purely masculine . . . While she touches the metaphysical soul of boxing, it is questionable whether she ever lays a glove on its heart . . . real men need more blood and guts.

Allen Fletcher, *Worcester Sunday Telegram*

## SERMONS AND SODA-WATER
### JOHN O'HARA
### 1960

The novellas represent no change in Mr. O'Hara's method. He normally puts everything into a novel, including the kitchen sink complete with stopped drain, plumber, and plumber's mate, and does this not once but four or five times per book. The novella form has merely limited the author in a statistical way; one kitchen sink is all he can fit into his predetermined space . . .

*Atlantic Monthly*

## THE BIG LAUGH
### JOHN O'HARA
### 1962

When O'Hara is good he is very, very good; when he is bad he is writing for Hollywood . . . an exercise in tedium.

*New York Herald Tribune*

## THE HORSE KNOWS THE WAY
### JOHN O'HARA
### 1964

One might suggest . . . that the inhabitants of hell be condemned to an eternity reading stories behind the headlines in American tabloids . . . John O'Hara's new collection of short stories brings the whole realm uncomfortably close. It is a punishment to read . . .

*Christian Science Monitor*


## LOOK BACK IN ANGER
### JOHN OSBORNE
### 1956

. . . sets up a wailing wall for the latest post-war generation of under-thirties. It aims at being a despairing cry but achieves only the stature of a self-pitying snivel.

*Evening Standard*


## INADMISSIBLE EVIDENCE
### JOHN OSBORNE
### 1964

Before the end a feeling obtrudes that a bulldozer is being used where a trowel would have done.

Philip Hope-Wallace, *The Guardian*


## THE MESSIAH OF STOCKHOLM
### CYNTHIA OZICK
### 1987

. . . the novel's simple plot lines suddenly grow thick and tangled as jungle vines and the reader starts looking around for his machete. . . . messy and world hating.

*Buffalo News*

Reviewer devoured by jungle vines.

## THE LAST GENTLEMAN
### WALKER PERCY
### 1966

This is a curious, unfocused novel that rambles along with the wooden, almost arthritic, gait so often found in the work of writers who begin in middle age . . . indeed, it is difficult to see what precisely the author is at . . .

*New Republic*

## LOVE IN THE RUINS
### WALKER PERCY
### 1971

. . . some people are going to be embarrassed by an aging liberal's earnest attempt to write a youth cult novel.

*Library Journal*

## THE HOMECOMING
### HAROLD PINTER
### 1965

He is more cruel, gruesome and deliberately offensive in this two-act horror than in his previous plays. On its face value, it is callous and empty enough: what lies in its Freudian depths one dreads to think.

*Yorkshire Post*

## ZEN AND THE ART OF MOTORCYCLE MAINTENANCE
### ROBERT PIRSIG
### 1974

. . . a book full of grandiose promises and undelivered goods.

*Commentary*

## THE BELL JAR
### SYLVIA PLATH
### 1971

Highly autobiographical and . . . since it represents the views of a girl enduring a bout of mental illness, dishonest.

*Atlantic Monthly*

## OUT OF MY LEAGUE
### GEORGE PLIMPTON
### 1961

At first thought this seems flimsy substance for a real, live, grown-up book. It turns out that it is.

*San Francisco Chronicle*

## A LONG AND HAPPY LIFE
### REYNOLDS PRICE
### 1962

Very nearly a parody of the Southern Gothic novel . . . written in imitation Faulkner—a wearisome and hopeless style.

Whitney Balliett, *The New Yorker*

## V.
### THOMAS PYNCHON
### 1963

Reading *V.* is like listening to a scholarly but erratic documentation of Hell by a disinterested onlooker, while verbal sewage and vignettes of all that is most disgusting in mankind alternates with sociological asides, sardonic and blasphemous attacks on Christianity, Freudian tidbits. . . . To attempt to convey a sense of how completely boring all this melee finally is would tax the capabilities of better reviewers than myself.

*Best Sellers*

## THE CRYING OF LOT 49
### THOMAS PYNCHON
### 1966

. . . a curiously dead novel.

*Book Week*

## SHAKESPEARE'S DOG
### LEON ROOKE
### 1983

Anyone interested in conventional novels with character and plot will want to let the neighbor's mongrel chew on *Shakespeare's Dog.*

*Books In Canada*

Ch. Hamlet of Stratford-on-Avon, CDX

## PORTNOY'S COMPLAINT
### PHILIP ROTH
### 1969

This looks and sounds like a Jewish novel. It isn't. Or, if it is, it is not a good one, a true one . . . it is finally a definitive something or other. I regret that it is not a definitive something.

*America*

The best that can be said of Roth's accomplishment is that Mama Portnoy is a caricature drawn by a master cartoonist, but she's not more than that. . . . The main trouble with the Jewish family theme is that it has been overwritten.

*The Nation*

## OUR GANG
### PHILIP ROTH
### 1971

Nixon's rough treatment at Roth's hands may very well invite more sympathy for him than anything since the Checker's speech.

*Saturday Review*

# THE GREAT AMERICAN NOVEL
## PHILIP ROTH
### 1973

Roth has, most unfortunately, got into such a shouting match with his readers that some of us are going to have to start shouting back.

*Encounter*

# MY LIFE AS A MAN
## PHILIP ROTH
### 1974

. . . a totally solipsistic novel, which may well make it a perfect expression of the times . . .

*Commentary*

# FRANNY AND ZOOEY
## J.D. SALINGER
### 1961

. . . cute.

Alfred Kazin, *Atlantic Monthly*

## RAISE HIGH THE ROOF BEAM CARPENTER AND SEYMOUR: AN INTRODUCTION
### J.D. SALINGER
### 1963

. . . not even a writer of Salinger's stature—and he is our only authentic living giant—can make a god out of a suicide.

*America*

Hopelessly prolix . . .

*New York Times Book Review*

## CRUCIAL CONVERSATIONS
### MAY SARTON
### 1976

May Sarton's book reads like an unsuccessful attempt to make a Montaigne out of a molehill.

*The Listener*

## THE HOUSE BY THE SEA
### MAY SARTON
### 1977

I think her lack of greater popularity is due to her habit of dissecting her bowels and displaying them for public observation.

*Maine Life*

Maine, 1977 — the first bookectomy.

## THE MAGNIFICENT SPINSTER
MAY SARTON
1986

The experience of the book, personally speaking, was like a long hike home in wet socks and gym shoes, uncomfortable and unnecessary.

*Out*

## AMADEUS
PETER SHAFFER
1981

. . . The New York audience, the night I went, gave the play a standing ovation. A cynical friend maintains that Broadway audiences always do this to justify to themselves the mountainous cost of the evening out . . .

Robert Cushman, *Observer*

## ROUGH STRIFE
LYNNE SHARON SCHWARTZ
1981

. . . almost wholly uninteresting.

*Times* (London)

. . . unintentionally hilarious.

*Village Voice*

## DISTURBANCES IN THE FIELD
LYNNE SHARON SCHWARTZ
1983

. . . a fat, shapeless, talky, self-satisfied blob of a book.

*Washington Post Book World*

## LAST EXIT TO BROOKLYN
HUBERT SELBY
1965

This is Grove Press's extra special dirty book for fall . . .

*Time*

## THE AUTOBIOGRAPHY OF UPTON SINCLAIR
UPTON SINCLAIR
1963

The book's value is limited, unless of course there is a socialist temperance league around somewhere.

*Critic*

## THE BENEFACTOR
SUSAN SONTAG
1963

Mrs. Sontag is an intelligent writer who has, on her first flight, jettisoned the historical baggage of the novel. However, she has not replaced it with material or insights that carry equal or superior weight. . . . Instead she has chosen the fashionable imports of neo-existentialist philosophy and tricky contemporary techniques.

*New York Times Book Review*

## DEATH KIT
SUSAN SONTAG
1967

. . . participates in the dull listlessness of its theme; it becomes the ennui it describes.

*Christian Science Monitor*

## THE GIRL HUNTERS
MICKEY SPILLANE
1963

A sorry exhibit of toughness gone slimy.

*New Statesman*

## POETS ON POETRY
### WILLIAM STAFFORD
### 1986

. . . probably the most puzzlingly destructive and unwittingly dismissive book about poetry by a poet that has ever been written.

*Ironwood*

## THE SPECTATOR BIRD
### WALLACE STEGNER
### 1976

This is a dreary, contrived, mercifully short novel . . . It would seem that Stegner emptied a desk drawer and decided to make a book out of the contents. . . . This book is recommended only to the most ardent Stegner fans, and preferably those with masochistic tendencies.

*Monterey Peninsula Herald*

## THE WINTER OF OUR DISCONTENT
### JOHN STEINBECK
### 1961

It is regrettable that the author . . . has invested the book with a lot of mumbo-jumbo and hocus-pocus involving a talisman, a female witch and ambiguous religious significance that results in a contrived pretentious story . . .

*Catholic World*

This is clearly a comeback effort, and just as clearly a failure.

*New Republic*

## SET THIS HOUSE ON FIRE
### WILLIAM STYRON
### 1960

. . . bathetic.

*Commonweal*

. . . a 507 page crying jag.

*Time*

## SCHIZOPHRENIA: THE SACRED SYMBOL
### THOMAS S. SZASZ
### 1976

Szasz blasts society with all the explosive force of a popgun.

Richard Jacoby, *The Nation*

## THE MYTH OF MENTAL ILLNESS
### THOMAS S. SZASZ
### 1962

The reviewer knows of no psychiatrist who agrees with Szasz and is sorry to consider his book a total waste of time.

*The Psychiatric Quarterly*

## THE PHENOMENON OF MAN
### PIERRE TEILHARD DE CHARDIN
### 1960

The attempt to turn the concept of evolution into a meta-physical key to the universe is one of the graveyards of the intellect, and the present work is merely one more testimony to that fact.

*Guardian*

## WHAT IS REMEMBERED
### ALICE B. TOKLAS
### 1963

Regrettably about all Miss Toklas remembers from her famous relationship with Gertrude Stein are cool rides and cerise girdles.

*Critic*

## THE MUSIC SCHOOL
### JOHN UPDIKE
### 1966

As a producer of short stories, he marks time, offering only the spillover from the ever-dripping adjectival faucet . . .

*Christian Science Monitor*

## RABBIT REDUX
### JOHN UPDIKE
### 1971

*Rabbit Redux* is bad in all the ways *Rabbit Run* was bad, but it is bad in some different ways as well. It is a tedious album of the most futile monochromes of Sixties America: it is leering, erratic, and gimmicky; it is disingenuous and trite. At best it is dull, at worst the shabby outrage of an imagination damaged by indulgence . . .

*Book World*

## MYRA BRECKINRIDGE
### GORE VIDAL
### 1968

. . . a rather damp fizzle.

*Library Journal*

## CREATION
### GORE VIDAL
### 1981

Vidal's book is manufactured, not created.

*New Statesman*

## BREAKFAST OF CHAMPIONS
### KURT VONNEGUT
### 1973

From time to time it's nice to have a book you can hate—
it clears the pipes—and I hate this book.

Peter Prescott, *Newsweek*

## SLAPSTICK,
## OR LONESOME NO MORE
### KURT VONNEGUT
### 1976

. . . a sorry performance, full of bored doodling.

Robert Towers, *New York Review of Books*

## THE GALAPAGOS KID
### LUKE WALTON
### 1971

. . . just terrible.

*Publishers Weekly*

## RAT MAN OF PARIS
### PAUL WEST
### 1986

All of this would make a great short story. Unfortunately, this is a 180 page novel.

*Bestsellers*

## THE KANDY-KOLORED, TANGERINE-FLAKE, STREAMLINED BABY
### TOM WOLFE
### 1965

One wants to say to Mr. Wolfe; you're so clever, you can write so well, tell us something interesting.

*Saturday Review*

## THE PAINTED WORD
### TOM WOLFE
### 1975

There is plenty of hot air in this particular balloon, but I don't see it going anywhere.

John Russell, *New York Times Book Review*

## REVOLUTIONARY ROAD
### RICHARD YATES
### 1961

There is a certain cheapness, even an intellectual dishonesty, in pretending that the suburbanites . . . are pseudo-vertebrates who bend in the middle when confronted by the pressures of living their own lives.

*New York Herald Tribune Lively Arts*

## MISS MACINTOSH, MY DARLING
### MARGUERITE YOUNG
### 1965

. . . In her zeal to demonstrate that nothing lives except in the imagination, Miss Young, with superb virtuosity, may have written a novel that in the profoundest sense does not exist.

Melvin Maddocks, *Christian Science Monitor*

# LETTERS

## JESSICA MITFORD

I adore the first edition of *Rotten Reviews* and see therein that my collateral forebear Mary Russell Mitford slanged Jane Austen—that was a pretty silly thing for her to have done.

One problem that you may have run into when selecting from contemporary reviews is that these days reviewers are so damn polite—or I think "balanced" is the word. So that while I've had many adverse reviews over the years, they don't really qualify as rotten . . .

The best I could come up with is the enclosed from the Congressional Record . . .

### WILLIAM STAFFORD

It has sometimes occurred to me that the literary world would be much improved if critics just wrote the literature in the first place, thus avoiding that roundabout process in which the author struggles inside the complex of his book, like Laocoon contending with myriad problems, while the critic whisks through the finished book in a few minutes and immediately spots the gross blunders the author has taken a year or more to make.

ANSEL ADAMS to WALLACE STEGNER
*(enclosing our reprinted review of* The Spectator Bird)

Dear Wally,

This kind of Krap reminds me of the classic rejoinder of a musician who got a bad criticism from the London *Times*.

Music Critic
London Times
London G.B.

Dear Sir:

I am sitting in a secluded small room of my apartment.

Your criticism is before me.
In a few minutes it will be behind me.

## Howard Nemerov

Thanks for the invitation to RRII. The enclosed is the most recent and accessible instance; it is from Kirkus Services. I dunno what I done to these people far back in the ages, but I wish I had done it harder.

## Edward Abbey

I've probably missed some good reviews of my work over the years, but never a bad one—some fellow author is always eager to tell me about the bad ones.

## John Hollander
*(on his review of Allen Ginsberg's* Howl*)*

This review was written in my youth and in a sort of worked-up high dudgeon which echoed the high-camp-prophetic mode of *Howl*'s front matter, and which may have masked some of my disappointment in a turn I saw an old friend and poetic mentor to have taken. I only regret now that I hadn't given "America" and "In a Supermarket in California" time to register; I should have certainly commended them. As for not foreseeing that Allen Ginsberg would provide so much hymnody and doctrine to the counterculture which was soon to emerge, I have no regrets, having no stake in prophecy.

### ROSELLEN BROWN

Alas, though I've had some pretty dumb and even offensive things said about my work, nobody's ever managed to be particularly interesting in their dispraise. Now I'm going to crawl off and contemplate whether that's my fault or not: perhaps I don't give them enough truly interesting openings. . .?

### GAY TALESE

I wonder about the wisdom of resurrecting these nitwit reviews—which, being forgotten and unsuccessful in their efforts to kill off a work, are left better alone in their obscure place, no? Also, I think the worst and most mean-spirited of book critics usually get appropriate rewards for their efforts: the reviewer who was the most personally vicious about my last book is now relegated to the unenviable task of reviewing daily television.

## LOUIS L'AMOUR

In the first place I do not believe writers should read reviews of their own books, and I do not. If one is not careful one is soon writing to please reviewers and not their audience or themselves. My wife occasionally reads a review to me but so far I've not had a really bad one or many would have told me . . .

I reviewed books for a time for a midwest newspaper, and afterward went into the army. One night when I was holding down the orderly room there was a telephone call asking for me. I admitted who I was, and it turned out to be an author whose book had not received a very good review from me. He said, "*Private* L'Amour, this is *Major* _____. I believe you reviewed a book of mine once."

However, he turned out to be a nice guy with no hard feelings, but for a few minutes there, he had me on my heels.

## Luke Walton

You mentioned in *Rotten Reviews* that you plan a second volume of reviews and you invited submissions. Well, I enclose one from *Publishers Weekly* but I'm not famous like your other authors. I quit writing after *Publishers Weekly* told me my first novel was "just terrible." Something broke, you see. I was 29 and I'd worked for ten years at that novel, and I didn't see the point of spending another ten years only to be told the same thing again. So I tend bar here in North Plainfield, New Jersey and try to encourage the other writers who come by now and then. We don't get many writers in North Plainfield.

Luke Walton toasts his reviewer.

Isaac Asimov

Like all writers, I fume at bad reviews, and a fellow writer (Lester del Rey) once gave me some very good advice.

"When you read a review," he said, "at the very first unfavorable adjective, read no more and throw it away."

I have done that faithfully and, as a result, I have no bad reviews to send to you.

I also throw away good reviews, by the way, but I read them first.

## Joyce Carol Oates

I have not, for obvious reasons, saved any of my multitude of "rotten reviews." This one,* though not terribly negative, just came in . . . If you think it too mild, or not outrageous, or funny, enough, maybe I could find something else. (Under a rock perhaps.) Or I could just sit back and wait for the barrage that will surely accompany my next novel.

*See *On Boxing*—ed.

## HAROLD BRODKEY

Here are some rotten reviews. I am ashamed these quotes are so stupid. I'd thought they were funnier.

## ERICA JONG

Since *Fear of Flying* is now a bonafide classic with ten million copies in print from Japanese to Serbo-Croat not to mention twenty other languages, this review does not have the *personal* sting it once had. Nevertheless, it broke my heart in 1974 and, in a way, is typical of the treatment fresh and radical books receive.

## JAMES ATLAS

No critic who has even been through the experience of getting slammed by reviewers as I have recently can ever feel quite the same about his job. You might still be sharp in your criticism, might still render a negative verdict, but any trace of anger, sarcasm, disparagement are banished forever. You're always aware of the reality of what you're doing, of the pain, even anguish your words might cause. As I look back on some of the harsher appraisals I rendered so blithely over the years, I think: how could you have said that? Well, the job has to get done; if I don't like a book, I'm still going to say so, though in a gingerly way and with genuine remorse. As a famous but often derided novelist once said to me: they think we can take it, but we can't.

# FOR THE BEST IN PAPERBACKS, LOOK FOR THE 🐧

In every corner of the world, on every subject under the sun, Penguin represents quality and variety—the very best in publishing today.

For complete information about books available from Penguin—including Pelicans, Puffins, Peregrines, and Penguin Classics—and how to order them, write to us at the appropriate address below. Please note that for copyright reasons the selection of books varies from country to country.

**In the United Kingdom:** For a complete list of books available from Penguin in the U.K., please write to *Dept E.P., Penguin Books Ltd, Harmondsworth, Middlesex, UB7 0DA.*

**In the United States:** For a complete list of books available from Penguin in the U.S., please write to *Dept BA, Penguin, 299 Murray Hill Parkway, East Rutherford, New Jersey 07073.*

**In Canada:** For a complete list of books available from Penguin in Canada, please write to *Penguin Books Canada Ltd, 2801 John Street, Markham, Ontario L3R 1B4.*

**In Australia:** For a complete list of books available from Penguin in Australia, please write to the *Marketing Department, Penguin Books Australia Ltd, P.O. Box 257, Ringwood, Victoria 3134.*

**In New Zealand:** For a complete list of books available from Penguin in New Zealand, please write to the *Marketing Department, Penguin Books (NZ) Ltd, Private Bag, Takapuna, Auckland 9.*

**In India:** For a complete list of books available from Penguin, please write to *Penguin Overseas Ltd, 706 Eros Apartments, 56 Nehru Place, New Delhi, 110019.*

**In Holland:** For a complete list of books available from Penguin in Holland, please write to *Penguin Books Nederland B.V., Postbus 195, NL–1380AD Weesp, Netherlands.*

**In Germany:** For a complete list of books available from Penguin, please write to *Penguin Books Ltd, Friedrichstrasse 10–12, D–6000 Frankfurt Main 1, Federal Republic of Germany.*

**In Spain:** For a complete list of books available from Penguin in Spain, please write to *Longman Penguin España, Calle San Nicolas 15, E–28013 Madrid, Spain.*